Preface

Phylum Mollusca comprises up to 60% of global biodiversity. It is the second largest invertebrate group next to insects. Molluscs are highly adaptive to environment in which they live. Class Gastropoda is the second largest class of molluscs, involving 80% of the known molluscs than the bivalves. Molluscan population is declining globally in spite of their large numbers. This phylum stands first in number of reported extinctions in recent times. Total diversity of non-marine molluscs of Karnataka is not documented but studies are confined to the diversity Western Ghats or particular localities.

This book gives the taxonomic status of gastropods and bivalves inhabiting the land and freshwater habitats of Karnataka. The information provided in this book is result of extensive field studies from freshwater habitats (rivers and paddy fields) and terrestrial habitats (Forests, Plantations, Nagabanas) of Karnataka. Besides, the book is expected to give broader picture on the molluscs inhabiting freshwater and terrestrial ecosystems of the state and pictorial guide for molluscan identification.

Non-marine molluscs face challenges in their ecosystems due to anthropogenic activities that lessens their biodiversity. Molluscs are facing threat due to overharvesting, construction of dams, mining and urban developments in the freshwater habitats. Anthropogenic disturbances viz. conversion of forests unto agricultural sites are major threat to land molluscs.

The objective of this book is to give collective account on documented nonmarine molluscs of Karnataka that will help layman, students, stake holders, conservationists to know about the diversity and to prioritize conservation action plans. The details on nonmarine molluscs of Karnataka may be helpful for researchers to carry out future research on these ecosystems.

This book gives details on 15 species freshwater molluscs and 20 land snail species of coastal Karnataka. Moreover, 3 land snail species collected during the field surveys from the Western Ghats are described here. Some of the freshwater molluscs are consumed locally viz. *Pila virens, Lamlelidens marginalis, Idiopoma* sp.

They are of medicinal importance too. For example *Pila* spp. are used for digestive ailments and to treat constipation. The Gaint African snail *Lissachatina fulica* is vector of parasites causing meningitis in humans and voracious feeder. Slugs such as *Mariella dussumeiri*, *Levicaulis alte* etc are pests to crops. This book is aimed to contribute to the taxonomy and conservation of non-marine molluscs of Karnataka.

My gratitude to Dr. K Bhasker Shenoy, Retired Professor, Department of Applied Zoology, Mangalore University for the guidance. Heartfelt thanks to the Fr. Vice Chancellor and staff of the Zoology department for their encouragement. I am extremely thankful to Dr. Venkitesan, Scientist E, Zoological Survey of India, Chennai, a n d Dr. Basudev Tripathy, Zoological Survey of India, Kolkata, Dr. Aravind Madhyastha, ATREE Bangalore for confirming the identity of molluscan shells.

I acknowledge the assistance of Mr Jayaram, Mrs. Baby, nonteaching staff of the department of Applied Zoology, Mangalore University during the study. Special thanks to Mr. Manjunath Hosabale for the help in collection of land snails.

Sandhya Leeda D'Souza

21.09.2024

Contents

Introduction

The coastal belt of Karnataka harbours seas, rivers, streams, reservoirs, ponds, lakes etc that are more productive in nature. Moreover, the man made paddy fields add to the scenic beauty of coastal Karnataka. The coast is known for the production of agricultural crops.Paddy is the main cereal crop grown in the wetlands of Karnataka. Kharif (April to October) and Rabi (December to March) crops are being cultivated in the coast according to the seasons. The terrestrial ecosystems of the Karnataka coast have sacred grooves, semi-forested regions plantations and gardens. The major crops grown in the plantations are banana, cashew, coconut, arecanut etc. Exotic trees such as acacia, Casurina, rubber are also seen in Karnataka coast. Casurina plantations are found near beaches of Dakshina Kannada and Uttara Kannada districts.

Phylum Mollusca is the second largest invertebrate group next to insects, and also largest marine phylum. More than 90,000 species of molluscs are known at the global level. The living classes of this phylum are Aplacophora (worm like shell less molluscs), Polyplacophora (chitons), Bivalvia (clams, mussels, oysters), Monoplacophora (rare deep sea molluscs),   Cephalopoda (squids, octopus, cuttle fish), Gastropoda (snails and slugs), Scaphopoda (tusk shells).

A total of 6688 species of molluscs are known from freshwater habitats of the world. Of these 212 molluscan species are documented from freshwater habitats of India. Highest number of molluscs species are confined to Western Ghats and to Eastern Himalayan hotspots (Tripathy and Mukhopadhyay, 2014). Among the 1487 species of land molluscs known from India, 79 species are reported from Karnataka (Madhyastha *et al.*, 2004).

Non-marine molluscs are found in a wide range of freshwater and terrestrial habitats, and highly adaptive to environment in which they live. They have different life-history strategies and exhibit complex ecological interactions, due to which they can be used in environmental assessment. They are the prominent links in the trophic levels, help in nutrient cycling in the environment and play significant roles in bio-geochemical cycles.

Based on their feeding habits molluscs are classified as herbivores (algal feeders) carnivores (on other invertebrates), parasites and scavengers (feeding on dead and decaying animals). Freshwater bivalves are filter feeders, filtering out phytoplanktons and zooplanktons, as well as bacteria and other particles, thus maintaining water quality.

Molluscs help in biomonitoring act as carriers of human-related parasites and diseases. Due to the good quality meat and protein contents freshwater mussels are suitable for human consumption. Mother of pearl is found inside freshwater mussels which can be used to make pearls, buttons and ornaments.

As vectors, freshwater molluscs such as *Racesina luteola, Indoplanorbis exustus, Gyraulus* spp. are the intermediate host of many trematodes, of which schistosomiasis is recognised need as a potential threat to human population. Molluscs are good models for studying animal biology, neurobiology and evolution. Freshwater molluscs are food for fishes. Larvae of freshwater mussels are called glochidia which remain as parasites in fishes. They use fins and gills of fishes as their host to get nourishment.

The outer most shell of snails is visible component of made up of calcium which aiding in protection, support and buoyancy. The structure of shell varies in different classes of molluscs. Hermaphroditism is common in molluscs but cross fertilization an also occur. Fertilization external or internal, development by producing the larvae or direct without larval stage.

Another group of non-marine molluscs are gastropods living in terrestrial habitats are the land snails, those without shells are known as slugs. They are characterised by a head, fleshy foot and paired tentacles (Ramakrishna and Mitra, 2002). More than 20,000 land snail species are described from the world. They occur in varied habitats from tropical rainforest to deserted habitats and alpine forests at higher elevation (Raheem *et al.*, 2009). They are found in moist places during monsoon, forested and semi-forested regions, invading the urban areas, agricultural sites, sacred grooves, nagabanas, home gardens etc. Nagabanas are called mini sacred groves covering an area of few cents to acres on rare occasions. Further, a small part of natural vegetation will be retained and devoted to local diety.

Shells of land snails are the most important structures used for their identification owing to their variation in size, shape, sculpture and texture (Mitra *et al.*, 2004). Usually, size of the shell in land snails ranges between 1-2mm to 80-100mm. Prosobranch snails possess an operculum which closes the shell aperture, whereas pulmonates lack an operculum (Ramakrishna and Mitra, 2002).

Based on the shell size, land snails can be categorised into two types namely, macrogastropods and microgastropods. Macro-gastropods are larger in body size, and fully grown shell having shell diameter of >5mm (Aravind *et al.*, 2008). Largest macrogastropods reach a maximum shell width of 13cm. Some of the examples are Gaint African snail, *Euplecta* sp, *Cyclophorous* sp etc. In India, micro-gastropods are known to represent 40% of the land snail diversity of the Western Ghats (Aravind *et al.*, 2008).

Land snails species of India viz. *Lissachatina fulica, Allopeas gracile, Macrochlamys* sp, *Ariophanta solita, Cryptozona semirltgata, Oryptozona bistrialis* and *Bensonia monticola* etc are pestiferous in nature. *Rachistia* sp, *Lissachatina fulica, Subulina octona* and *Allopeas gracile* are introduced species to India whereas *Gulella bicolor, Euplecta* sp, *Cyclphorous* sp, *Pterocyclus* sp are native land snails to India (Raut and Goose, 1984). Introduced land snail species increase in number by foraging on native plants. Thus, introduced land snails lessen the population of the native land snails (Jayashankar *et al.*, 2011). Land molluscs such as *Cycophrous* spp, *Gaint African snail, Spiraculum* spp. are widely consumed in West Bengal and North eastern parts of India (Aravind and Jadhav, 2023).

Non-marine molluscs are facing threat due to overharvesting, construction of dams, mining, deforestation, urban developments, flooding and conventional farming techniques in their habitats. Although the current research explores the biology and ecology of molluscs, future studies on molluscs need to concentrate on data collection by extensive sampling to discover the unexplored species and to understand their distribution. Conservation of non-marine molluscs should be prioritized based on threat status at species specific sites.

Taxonomy of Molluscs

Conchological features of the shell help in understanding the taxonomy and systematics of the molluscs. However, internal anatomical features, structure and dentition of radula, morphology of reproductive organs are used in species identifications. The shell of freshwater gastropods is single, offers a great number of characters useful in taxonomy. The general shape varies in different gastropod families. The presence or absence of an operculum, the number, and nature of coiling and shape of whorls, sculpture, the nature of umbilicus and columella, and the shape of the aperture in a shell are very important to a taxonomist.

Bivalve molluscs have two shells connected by ligaments and muscles. External shell characteristics are used in identification of taxa. Although freshwater mussels are predominately elongate-oval, shell variation is immense within and among species. A mantle that lines the shell is present, and isolates the internal organs from extra-visceral water.

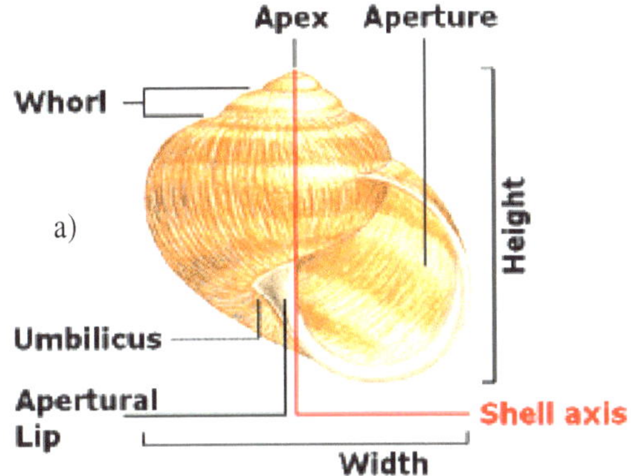

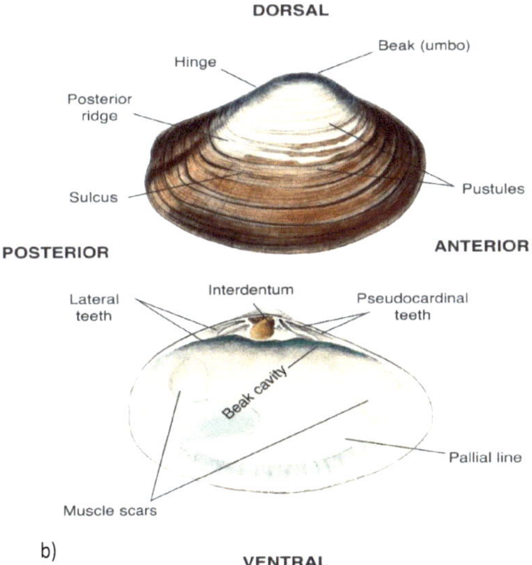

General body plan of molluscs: a. Gastropod, b. Bivalve

Shell shape:

Gastropod shell terminology can be illustrated with a spiral shell. The pointed end of the shell opposite the aperture is the apex. Shell length in spiral shells is measured form the apex to the lower tip of the aperture, while the greatest diameter is used in planospiral shells. The spire is separated into a number of whorls by sutures. The initial shell of a newly hatched snail is the most apical whorl. The final whorl represents the most recent growth and ends in the aperture from which the foot protrudes. If whorls are flat and placed one above the other tapering towards the tip, the shell is termed "cone-shaped." Moderately inflated whorls produce a sub-globose shell, and shells that are almost circular are globose.

The gastropods are characterized by shells that are helical, usually opening to the right, but to the left occasionally. Shape of the shell varies conical, globose (Ampullarids), or discoidal (Planorbidae). Freshwater "limpets" have a simple conical shell and the planorbid gastropods have a planospiral shell with the whorls all in one plane. The whorls are elevated in a spire in the molluscs belonging to pulmonate families, Physidae and Lymnaeidae and in caenogastropod families. In thiarids, such as *Melanoides tuberculata* shell is elongated conic, turreted, or ovate-conoidal, solid with spiral ridges and/or axial ribs. The turbinate shell form can be seen in shells like *Filopauludina* spp. having shape like a cone that rests on its apex. Whorls can be rounded and have deep sutures as in a typical lymnaeid shell.

Along with outer shell shape and its size, the internal shell structures are considered for the identification of freshwater bivalves. Ligament structures, muscle scar patterns, hinge teeth are taken into account for the classification of bivalves. Beyond this, classification relies on internal traits of the molluscs that is expected to help in understanding their evolutionary patterns. The cryptic species can be identified using the conchological characteristics, internal structures, at later stage molecular phylogeny at genetic level (Borges *et al.*, 2022).

Bivalves are usually have shells that are elongate-elliptical (*Lamellidens* spp.) or orbicular (*Corbicula* spp.) Shell thickness varies from thin and fragile, as in *Spherium indicum*, to thick and resistant-to-crushing, as in the caenogastropods.

Shell shapes of freshwater molluscs (Source:Aravind and Jadhav, 2023)

Morphological features of the slugs

Slugs are soft-bodied and slimy, and are generally vary in colour. They have two pairs of tentacles: Upper pair: Also known as the optical tentacles, these are the eyes of the slug. They have light-sensing eyespots at the end and can be re-grown if lost. Lower pair: These smaller tentacles are used for feeling and tasting. The saddle-shaped area is located behind the head of the slug is mantle. A large respiratory pore is present known as pneumostome usually found on the right side of the mantle.

Slugs move by rhythmic waves of muscular contraction on the underside of their foot. Most slugs have a remnant of their shell, internalized known as vestigial shell. This organ usually stores calcium salts. A ridge or keel is found that runs the length of the back of some species of slug. Tail is present behind the mantle.

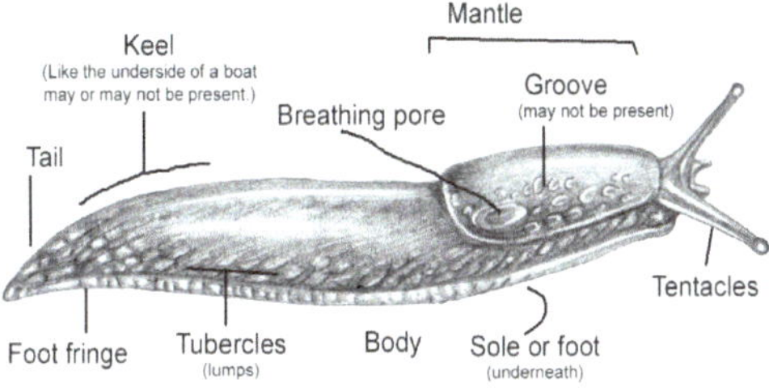

Body parts of a slug

Freshwater gastropods

Family: Ampullaridae

1. *Pila virens* (Lamarck, 1822)

Common name: Green Apple Snail

Shell size: Height =14-16 mm, Width=12mm, No. of whorls: 5.

Morphology: The colour can vary from uniform yellow-olive to dark brown. The shell surface is smooth in most cases, body whorl inflated with depressed spire, Sutures deeply impressed, Suture canaliculate with a distinct carination of the whorls on the outside, spire prominent and conical takes $1/4^{th}$ of the height of the shell. Apex is obtuse. Aperture ovate broad below. Peristome continuous with distinct lip that is tilted backwards and has the ridge for operculum to fit in. Very narrow umbilicus, partly hidden by retroverted inner lip, ovate and concentric operculum. Callus well developed. Body whorl swollen with irregular dark spiral bands.

Distribution: Restricted to Peninsular India in the Deccan region, Assam, south of river Krishna and Godavari river basin, Southern Karnataka.

Ecology: Species generalist tolerant to moderate levels of organic pollution and habitat disturbances.

Other highlights: Birds such as open billed storks prey on these species. It is an ideal candidate for heliciculture.

Pila virens: a) Abapertural view, b) Apertural view, Scale bar=8mm

Family: Viviparidae

2. *Melanoides tuberculata* (Muller, 1774)

Common name: Red-rimmed Melania, Malaysian trumpet snail

Shell size: Height =27 – 80 mm, Width=10mm, No. of whorls: 10-14.

Morphology: An elongate, conical shell with whorls, usually light brown marked with rust coloured spots. The spots are either irregularly distributed or longitudinally arranged on the surface. Shell with a high spire, moderately large body whorl. It has high spire 5 times the height of aperture. An operculum is present and has coarse striations spirally up the shell. Longitudinally arranged on the shell surface sculptured conspicuously with vertical ribs and spiral striae, distinct and raised on the upper whorls, but flatter on the lower ones.

Distribution: All over India.

Ecology: Red-rimmed melania can breed sexually or parthenogenically.

Melanoides tuberculata: a) Abapertural view, b) Apertural view, Scale bar=8mm

Family: Bellaminidae

3. *Filopaludina bengalensis* (Lamarck, 1822)

Common name: Banded pond snail

Shell size: Height =30-35mm, Width=22-25mm, No. of whorls: 6.

Morphology: Shell conical, tin, greenish, with fine growth lines, linear dark green bands are present across the shell. Spire conical, protoconch pointed. Whorls convex, smooth with minor decussate striations. Body whorl inflated, highly impressed suture, pointed at the tip, aperture sub-oval with thin lip. Oval operculum brownish in colour.

Distribution: All over India.

Ecology: Generalist tolerant to high levels of organic pollution and habitat disturbances.High reproductive capacity, viviparous.

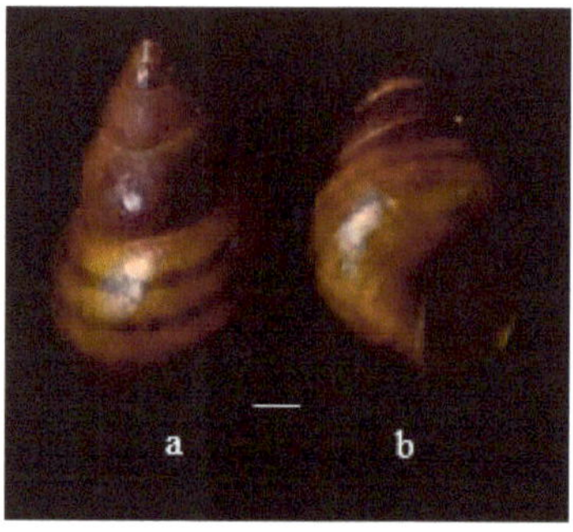

Filopaludina bengalensis: a) Abapertural view, b) Apertural view, Scale bar=8mm.

4. *Idiopoma dissimilis* (Muller, 1744)

Common name: Variable pond snail

Shell size: Height =32-36 mm, Width=18mm, No. of whorls=5-6.

Morphology: Shell small brownish in colour, Convex body whorl, elevated ridge, pale spiral band may or may not be present. Whitish riblets are present on the whorls running vertically. Umbilicus indistinct, Suture deeply impressed, Conical spire swollen, Aperture small and circular, thick operculum with concentric rings, exhibiting prominent muscle scar.

Distribution: All over India.

Ecology: Species generalist tolerant to moderate levels of organic pollution and habitat disturbances. High reproductive capacity.

Idiopoma dissimilis: a) Abapertural view, b) Apertural view, Scale bar =8mm

Family: Lymnaeidae

5. *Racesina luteola* (Lamarck, 1822)

Shell size: Height =18-20 mm, Width=10-11mm, No. of whorls=4-5.

Morphology: Shell thin, variable in colour, spire pointed longer, gradually tapering, body whorl less inflated laterally compressed. Oval aperture narrows above, nearly 2/3rd of shell height.

Distribution: Throughout South East Asia, Netravathi and Sharavthi rivers, Paddy field of Marlimar (Dakshina Kannada dist.) and Sastan (Udupi dist.) of coastal Karnataka.

Ecology: Survival capacity in low oxygen conditions and polluted water. They are either attached to aquatic vegetation or floating on the surface. Prolific breeders, dispersal through aquatic vegetation and birds. Young ones undergo dormancy during dry season.

Other highlights: Vector causing schistosomiasis, infecting human and cattle.

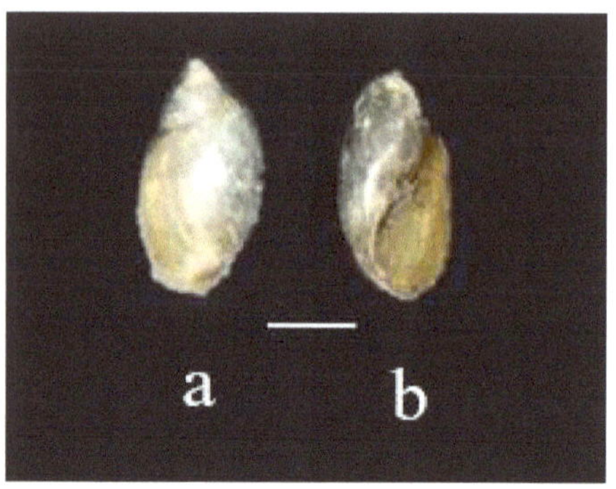

Racesina luteola: a) Abapertural view, b) Apertural view, Scale bar =8mm

Family: Thiaridae

6. *Mieniplotia scabra* (Müller, 1774)

Shell size: Height =10mm, Width=40mm, No. of whorls=5-6.

Morphology: Shells are highly polymorphic. Body colour white to brown, and may have dark straight or zig-zag lines. Shell elongate, turreted whorls regularly increasing in size; spire a: high as body whorl; sutures distinct, whorl often shouldered above and rounded below the row of spines; sculptured with vertical ribs bearing prominent spines directed obliquely outward, surface with rough spiral striations, on the body whorl near the umbilical region striations form strong ridges, pale brown in colour. The operculum is oval and paucispiral.

Distribution: All over India.

Ecology: Detritus and algal feeder.

Other highlights: *Mieniplotia* females are parthenogenetic and reproduce by releasing at a fairly advanced stage of hatching as crawling juveniles and carry a varying number of embryos in the brood pouch.

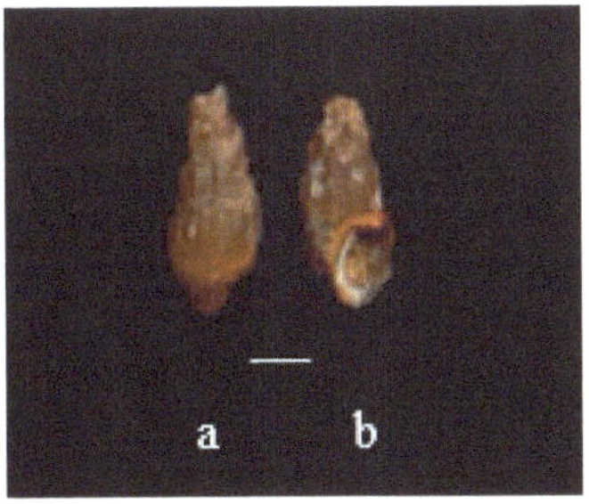

Mieniplotia scabra: a) Abapertural view, b) Apertural view, Scale bar =8mm

Family: Pachychilidae

7. *Brotia costula* (Rafinesque, 1833)

Common name: Cap snail

Shell size: Height =52-55 mm, Width=15-18mm, No. of whorls=6-12.

Morphology: Elongated shell, medium to large size, olive to green, sometimes bluish in colour. This sp. shows morphological variation on the shell. Spiral ridges or nodules are seen with prominent axial ribs on the whorls. Tip of the spire is often eroded. Impressed suture, Wide and rounded aperture at the base covering one fifth of the shell.

Distribution: Gangetic plains, Brahmaputra river basin, North-East India, Sharavathi and Netravathi rivers of Karnataka.

Other highlights: Found in clean water, intolerant to pollution.

Brotia costula: a) Abapertural view, b) Apertural view, Scale bar =8mm.

8. *Sulcospira huegeli* (Philippi, 1841)

Shell size: Height =6mm, Width=7mm, No. of whorls=5-6.

Morphology: Shell ovoid conical; spice generally decorated, whorls regularly increasing in size, body whorl large, almost equal to the height of the spire; sculpture nearly smooth, with spiral striae below the periphery of the body whorl; aperture vertical and produced at the base, dark brown.

Distribution: Assam, Karnataka Upper Cauvery River, Bangalore Kerala, Cochin Hills; Meghalaya: Khasi and Garo Hills.

Other highlights: Feeds on succulent vegetation.

Sulcospira huegeli: a) Abapertural view, b) Apertural view, Scale bar =8mm

Family: Physidae

9. *Physella acuta* (Draparnaud, 1805)

Common name: Bladder snail

Shell size: Height =15mm, Width=11mm, No. of whorls=5.

Morphology: Shells sinistral, the shells of *Physella* species have a long and large aperture, a pointed spire, and no operculum. Shell moderate, ovate, transparent but thick and sharply pointed apex; spire sharp and pointed; sutures oblique; body whorl large and around; sculpture smooth; aperture ovate.

Distribution: India.

Ecology: Well adapted to undergo anhydrobiosis

Other highlights: Non-native species, higher rate of fecundity. Depends on environmental conditions of the paddy fields for their survival. Tolerant to extreme temperature and water pollution.

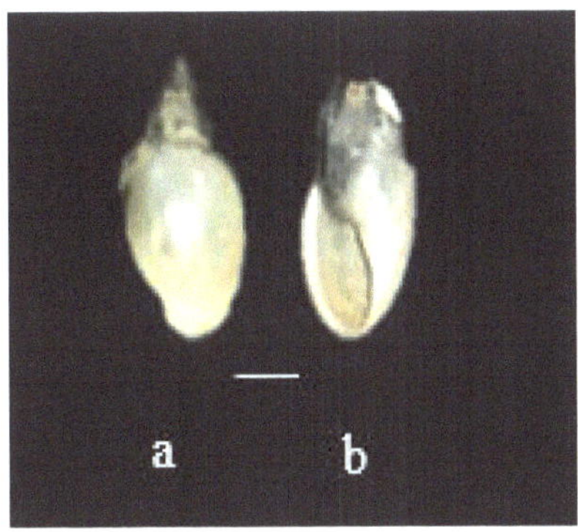

Physella acuta: a: Abapertural view, b: Apertural view, Scale bar =8mm

10. *Indoplanorbis exustus* (Deshayes, 1833)

Common name: Ram's horn snails.

Shell size: Height =10mm, Width=16 mm, No. of whorls=5.

Morphology: Shell large, discoidal, rounded at periphery, aperture ear shaped, suture deeply impressed. Dorso-ventrally flat and, sinistral in coiling, Discoid with rapidly increasing whorls. Ear-shaped aperture.

Distribution: Widely distributed in South East Asia, paddy fields of Dakshina Kannada and Udupi districts of coastal Karnataka.

Ecology: Intermediate host for trematodes in cattle (Gauffre-Autelin *et al.*, 2017)

Other highlights: Prolific breeders, Dispersal through birds and vegetation.

Indoplanorbis exustus: a: Apical view. b: Basal view, Scale bar =8mm

Freshwater bivalves

Family: Unionidae

1. *Parreysia favidens* (Benson, 1862)

Shell size: Length 43 mm, height 32 – 49.5 mm.

Morphology: Shell rounded thick, convex, brownish in colour inflated with zigzag ribs on the beak, unequilateral and angulate both on anterior and posterior margins, margins are wavy, cardinal teeth strong and broad.

Distribution: All over India.

Ecology: This sp. can be used as a biological indicator of polonium-210 in riverine systems.

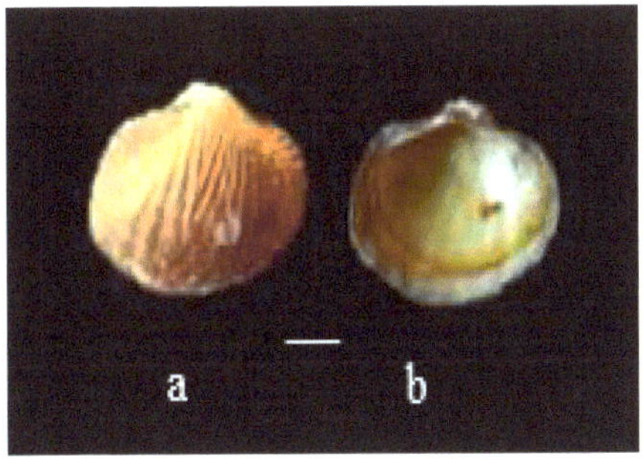

Parreysia favidens: a) Dorsal view, b) Ventral view, Scale bar: 5mm

2. *Parreysia corrugata* (Muller, 1774)

Shell size: Height =40-42mm, Width=30mm.

Morphology: Shell smooth. Green in colour, elliptic to oval, inequilateral, umbones prominent, sculptured with radiating, oblique, linear ridges ventral margin convex, lunule well marked, cardinal teeth strong, not lamellar. White in colour inside, pallial sinus clear, Umbonal region sometimes faded.

Distribution: All over India

Ecology: Tolerant to certain degree of pollution.

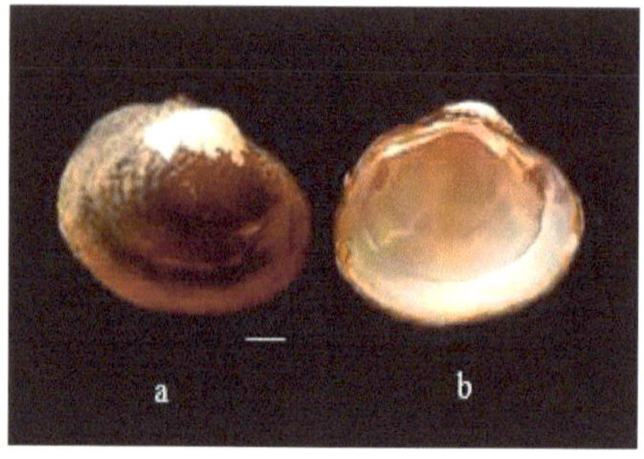

Parreysia corrugata: a) Dorsal view, b) Ventral view, Scale bar: 5mm

3. *Lamellidens marginalis* (Lamarck, 1819)

Shell size: Height=50mm, Length =85-90mm

Morphology: Shell oblong, ovate covered with blackish brown periostracum, with light brown border along the ventral margin, Inner surface of the shell is smooth, pearly in colour with a faint bluish tinge. Umbo prominent, not elevated, posterior side broad, angular, dorsal margin slightly curved, central margin slightly contracted in the middle, hinge with two cardinals in the right valve, interior nacreous. Muscle scars are present on the inner surface of the shell.

Distribution: All over India

Ecology: Filter feeder and detritivore .Tolerant to moderate levels of pollution.

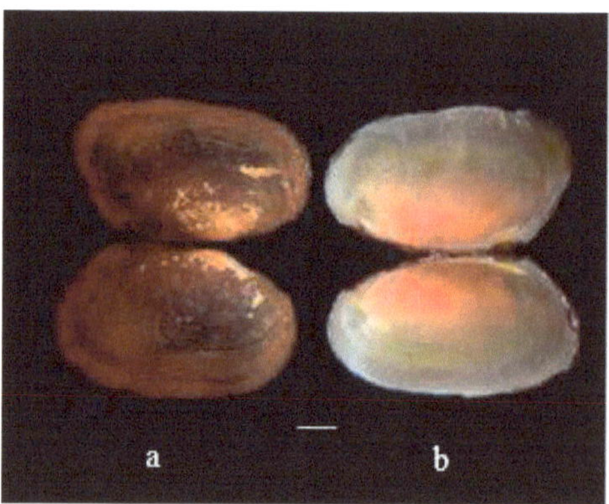

Lamellidens marginalis: a) Dorsal view, b) Ventral view, Scale bar: 5mm

Family: Sphaeriidae

4. *Spherium indicum* (Deshayes, 1854)

Common Name: Fingernail clams

Shell size: Max. 10mm in length

Morphology: Shell small rounded, fragile, pinkish white in colour, equilateral, their shells exhibit striae, thin parallel rows of elevated lines. Umbones median.

Distribution: Netravathi river of Karnataka

Ecology: Bio-indicator species sensitive to higher level of pollution. They are tolerant of anoxic conditions. Feeds on algae and phytoplanktons.

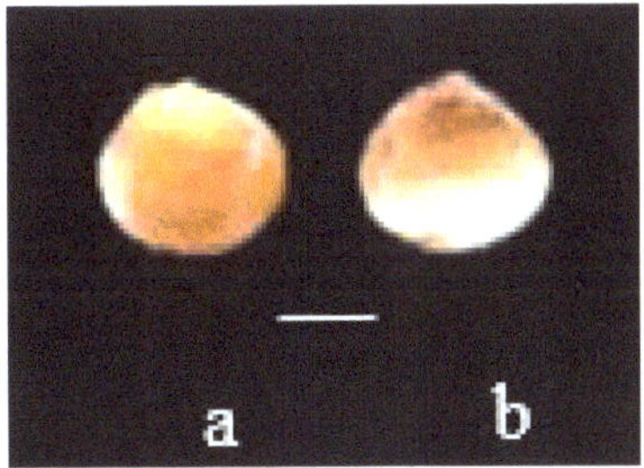

Spherium indicum: a) Dorsal view, b) Ventral view, Scale bar: 5mm

Family: Cyrenidae

5. *Corbicula striatella* (Deshayes, 1855)

Shell size: Height=15mm, Length=17.5-18.5mm

Morphology: Thick medium sized shell, triangularly ovate, dorsal margin arched more on anterior side, shining periostracum lemon yellow in juveniles brownish in adult shells, regular, concentric striae raised into ridges, pallial line with trace of sinus, well developed muscle scars.

Distribution: All over India.

Ecology: Tolerant to moderate levels of pollution and habitat disturbances.

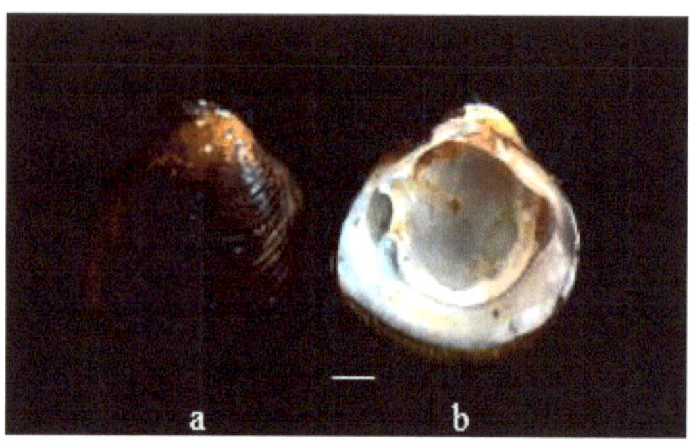

Corbicula striatella: a) Dorsal view, b) Ventral view, Scale bar: 5mm

List of freshwater molluscs of reported from coastal Karnataka.

SI. No	Species	Habitat	Uses (Aravind and Jadhav, 2023)
Gastropods			
1	*P. virens*	Streams, ponds, paddy fields	Food, medicine, research purposes
2	*M. tuberculata*	Living on the bottom sediments of rivers, Small springs lakes	Not known
3	*F. bengalensis*	Lentic and lotic water bodies	Widely consumed, Research, Heliciculture
4	*I. dissimilis*	Streams, ponds, paddy fields	Snail farming
5	*R. luteola*	Temporary or permanent stagnant water bodies, manmade habitats	Used as food, medicine and for trading in West Bengal, Research
6	*M. scabra*	Slow moving and stagnant waters.	Not known

7	*S. huegeli*	Fast running rivers and streams or lakes	Not known
8	*B. costula*	Streams, rivers with sandy bottoms, rocky bottoms occasionally. Lentic and lotic habitats.	Medicine in Northeast India, Poulty feed.
9	*P. acuta*	Paddy fields, polluted water, irrigation channels, dams, and streams	Not known
10	*I. exutus*	Stagnant waters	Not known

Bivalves

1	*P. favidens*	Found in the silt of rivers and streams	Consumed as food
2	*P. corrugata*	Lentic and lotic habitats, found buried in substratum	Consumed as food, used in handicraft industries
3	*L. marginalis*	Burrows in rivers	Food, medicine, pearl culture, lime production, used in research
4	*S. indicum*	Found burrowing in sediments of rivers and streams	Not known
5	*C. striatella*	Low land rivers, streams, lakes	Food, Research

*IUCN status of the species listed above is Least concerned.

Land molluscs

Family: Ariophantidae

1. *Mariaella dussumieri* (Gray, 1855).

Shell size: Length=46 mm.

Morphology: Shell internal, flat, solid in mature forms, with beak like apex, sides sharp, hay yellow in colour, spire indistinct. Yellowish with dark brown spots present in the hind region in older forms, the spots are not distinct in the younger. Shell is internal, partly visible, externally through the pore present on the top of the mantle. Mantle lobes united to form a shield enclosing the various systems, on the surface with two ridges running almost parallel to each other, the right one from the respiratory orifice to the shell aperture the other round the left margin. Posterior portion sharply keeled behind the mantle, ending in the mucus pore. Foot tripartite, edges with short vertical black parallel lines.

Distribution: Western Ghats, Maharashtra; Karnataka.

Ecology: It is an agricultural pest, feeding on all kinds of plants.

2. *Macrochlamys indica* (Godwin-Austen, 1883)

Shell size: Height=8-11mm, Width=12-15mm, No. of whorls=5-6
Morphology: Shell moderately large, depressed, perforate, thick, smooth, pale brownish, faintly decussately sculptured both above and below; spire low, conoid; whorls, convex, above, the last rounded above and below; aperture sub-vertical, widely lunate, peristome thin, columella curved, a little expanded and reflected above. Differs from other *Macrochlamys* sp. being larger thicker, the whorls being more rounded above and also being decussately sculptured.
Distribution: Throughout India.

3. *Macrochlamys* sp.

Shell size: Height=10mm, Width= 12mm, Whorls=3
Morphology: Resembles *M. indica* in morphology, Shell orange to brown in colour. Body of the animal is bluish to blackish in colour. Dextral shell, Body whorl id large than the others, spire prominent, aperture triangular.

Distribution: All over India.

4. *Euplecta indica* (Pfeiffer, 1846)

Shell size: H= 9 mm, W= 22 mm, whorls 5 - 6

Morphology: Shell sub-turbinate, lenticular, rather solid, perforate, fulvous throughout, ornamented above with slightly arcuate costulation, decussated by impressed spiral lines, which are often obsolete, each rib bearing raised points or granules at sub-equal distances; whorls slowly increasing, convex, the last keeled, smooth beneath and radiately striated below the keel, lower surface moderately swollen; spire conoid, with convex sides, aperture oblique, angularly lunate; peristome white, columellar margin oblique, curved, briefly reflexed above.

Distribution: Western Ghats, Karnataka, Annamalai, Nilgiris, Palani Hills; Kerala.

5. *Euplecta acuducta* (Benson, 1850)

Shell size: H= 15-20 mm, W= 25mm, No. of whorls=6

Shell light brown, whorls coiled around the central axis, slowly increasing, Keeled between the whorls, Brownish blotches are present on the shell, aperture rounded, columella straight, Umbilicus rounded, Spire pointed.

Distribution: Western Ghats, Karnataka: Dakshina Kannada, Karwar, Sharavathi Valley.

6. *Ariophanta immerita* (Blanford, 1870)

Shell size: H= 32 mm, W= 38 mm, Whorls 5.

Morphology: Shell sinistral, moderately umbilicate, thin, fragile, and translucent. Apex obtuse, dark brown above with a whitish band at the periphery after which the colour fades into white nearing the umbilicus, whorls rapidly increasing, and sutures not impressed. Shell surface with smooth transverse striations on body whorl distinctly angled, rounded near the aperture in mature forms; it takes the appearance of a keel in younger forms. Body whorl near the aperture scarcely descending, with nacre just behind the slight pinkish aperture, lips slightly thickened. Upper lip flattened, basal lip inflated and rounded, columellar lip triangularly reflected, but does not cover the comparatively wider umbilicus.

Distribution: Endemic to Western Ghats, Karnataka: Sagar.

7. *Allopeas gracile* (Hutton, 1834)

Shell size: Height=9.8 mm-12.1 mm; Width= 2.9-3.3 mm, No. of whorls=12

Morphology: The shell is conically elongated and slender, with a translucent, glossy surface of pale yellowish hue. It comprises 7½ to 8 whorls, tapering gradually towards a blunt apex. The protoconch consists of approximately two smooth whorls, while the subsequent whorls are adorned with obliquely arranged, fine, and densely packed riblets. The spire tapers evenly, and the whorls are flatly convex with a wide, shallow suture. The last whorl is the largest. The aperture is tall and oblong, with a thin peristome. The columellar margin near the umbilicus is slightly expanded, and the columella is straight. The umbilicus is narrowly open.

Distribution: All over India.

8. *Subulina octona* (Bruguière, 1789)

Common Name: Miniature Awl snail

Shell size: Height=14-17 mm, Width=3mm, No. of whorls= 8-9.

Morphology: The shell is long and narrow with a small, ovate aperture. The shell of this species is thin, translucent and glossy. The colour ranges from colorless to pale yellow-brown. The body of the animal is pale yellow. This species may be confused with *Allopeas gracile*; however, *Subulina octona* is larger and has a truncated columella.

Ecology: An intermediate host for three parasites.

Family: Alycaeidae

9. *Dicharax expatriatus* (Blanford and Blanford, 1860)

Shell size: Height= 5mm, Width=3-7mm, No. of whorls= 4

Morphology: The shell is small, rather depressed, being more strongly depressed in the spire. The surface of the shell is finely and closely transpirally grooved throughout. The body whorl bears a wide depressed area behind the peristome. This depression is traversed by a broad, tumid, ridge-like swelling· which is sharper and more well marked in certain nearly allied species, but is relatively blunt in the few specimens. The aperture is circular and oblique, and the peristome continuous, with a thin, duplicated margin, and markedly recurved at the point where it meets the penultimate whorl. The sutural tube is moderately long, but its length is subject to considerable individual variation. The umbilicus is fairly large and deep. The shell is dull whitish or creamy white, the apical whorls being reddish brown. The operculum is horny, distinctly multispiral, and externally concave, the central nucleus being internally prominently papillated.

Distribution: Neddoowuttom Ghat, Annamalais, Dakshina Kannada and Shevroy Hills; north of the Nilgiris and a little above the village of Goodaloor.

Family: Veronicellidae

10. *Laevicaulis alte* **(Ferussac, 1822)**

Common name: Tropical Leather leaf slug

Morphology: It is a round, dark-coloured slug with no shell, 7 or 8 cm long. Its skin is slightly tuberculated. The central keel is beige in colour. This slug has a unique, very narrow foot; juvenile specimens have a foot 1 mm wide and adult specimens have a foot that is only 4 or 5 mm wide. The tentacles are small, 2 or 3 mm long, and they are only rarely extended beyond the edge of the mantle.

Distribution: Throughout India.

Ecology: This slug is an intermediate host for *Angiostrongylus cantonensis*, the rat lungworm, causing of eosinophilic meningoencephalitis. It is a pest to horticulture.

Family: Cyclophoridae

11. *Micraulax coeloconus* **(Benson, 1851)**

Shell size: Height= 7-10mm, Width=13-14.5 mm

Morphology: Shell coiled, openly and widely umbilicate, with raised rib around the umbilicus, brownish, with zig-zag chocolate markings, also covered by a rough epidermis, obliquely striate by close coarse lines of growth; sutures crenulate, whorls convex; the last whorl sub inflated, wide; aperture oblique, sub circular, angulate above at the point of attachment to the last whorl.

Distribution: Dakshina Kannada, Western Ghats.

12. *Pterocyclus nanus* (Benson, 1851)

Shell size: Height=30-35mm, Width=35-38mm, No. of Whorls=6

Morphology: The shell is depressed, sub-discoidal, deeply and openly umbilicated. The whorls are narrow and rounded with very fine, obliquely transpiral striations on the surface. The aperture is oblique and circular, and the peristome is expanded into a thin, wing-like dilatation which is continuously swollen and bent forwards, overhanging the characteristic incision in the lip at this part. The shell is whitish, irregularly streaked and blotched all over with reddish brown markings. On the body whorl and the lower part of the spire these markings are more or less transpirally disposed, but they break up into irregular patches towards the spire. The lower surface of the shell is whitish, but is broadly banded with pale brown immediately surrounding the umbilicus.

Distribution: Western Ghats of Karnataka, Nilgiris, Anamalais; Southern India, Salem.

Cyclophorus spp.

13. *Cyclophorus* sp 1.

14. *Cyclophorus* sp 2.

Shell size: Height=40mm, Width=58-60mm, No. of whorls=5

Morphology: Shell much larger, rounded body whorl, reflected peristome, widely open umbilicus, spiral striae are seen on the shell, aperture oblique, circular, peristome orange red, expanded. Brownish bands are present on the shell.

Uses: These are consumed by Adi tribes in Arunachal Pradesh.

Family: Achatinidae

15. *Rishetia* sp. (Godwin-Austen, 1920)

Shell   Size: Height=50-55mm,   Width=4mm,   No.   of   whorls=12
Morphology: *Rishetia* has a stronger sculpture than *Glessula*. Shell elongately turreted, colour ruddy, regularly sculptured. The first whorl pointed with distinct and regular radial riblets, more prominent on the first few whorls, ribs much stronger towards the suture; middle whorls

of the shell show incised radial striation. Suture shallow, sides moderately flat. Aperture small, oval, peristome thin, columellar margin slightly convex, thinly calloused, white.

Distribution: Northeast India, Assam, Karnataka, Western Ghats.

16. *Lissachatina fulica* **(Bowdich, 1822)**

Common Name: Gaint African snail

Shell Size: Height=98.12mm, Width=50.55mm, No. of whorls=7

Morphology: Shell large, smooth, thin, conical twice as high as broad. Shell with continuous bands which are reddish brown to dark brown that runs around spirally. Body whorl moderately swollen with sharp conical spire. Whorls are convex with impressed sutures. Outer lip usually sharp and thin, Columella is more or less concave. Callus not prominent. Aperture elongate.

Distribution: All over India

Ecology: Found in tropical climates, warm and humid environments. Highly invasive species feeding more than 500 species of pants. Poses threat to native fauna and agriculture. This species is also an intermediate host of human lungworm *Angiostongylus cantonensis* which causes meningitis in humans (Mitra *et al.*, 2004).

Uses: Food in West Bengal.

Glessula von Martens, 1860,

17. *Glessula* sp.1

18. *Glessula* sp.2

Shell Size: Height=6.00 - 37.00 mm, Width=10-15mm. No. of Whorls=7-9

Morphology: Shell smooth, glossy, ovate-conic or turreted, faintly striate, columella abruptly truncate at base Shell, with or without spiral lirae on the first 1-2 whorls, first whorl rounded, body whorl broad.

Distribution: All over India.

19. *Guella bicolor* **(Hutton, 1834)**

Shell Size: Height=5-7mm, Width=2mm, No. of Whorls=8

Morphology: Shell small, elongate, imperforate, sub cylindrical-turreted, yellowish-white, smooth, faintly vertically striate, apex obtuse; whorls, little convex, sutures deep and crenulate, last whorl rounded at base, strongly indented on both sides forming deep pits; aperture vertical, semi-oval, truncate above, opening obliterated by four teeth, one parietal, One peristomal, one basal and one columellar, one fold obliquely running inward peristome, expanded and reflected, curved into a sinus on the right above.

Distribution: Common throughout India.

Ecology: Omnivorous snail feeding on plants, fungi and smaller land snails.

20. *Rachistia praetermissus* (Blanford, 1861)

Shell Size: H= 13 mm, W= 20 mm, No. of whorls -7.

Morphology: Shell narrowly umbilicate, oblong, conic, thin, striated, yellowish white, with two discontinuous bands and another continuous at the periphery, below which near the umbilicus it is fully chestnut coloured; occasionally white throughout, spire conic, apex acute, generally black. Whorls convex, last whorl more than the spire height. Aperture oblique or nearly ovate, peristome simple, upright, columellar margin vertical, arches reflexed. The tumid body whorl and the very delicate shell distinguish this species. The upper two bands are discontinuous and present on the penultimate whorl also.

Distribution: Western Ghats: Karnataka: Dandeli, B. R. Hills, Sharavathi Valley, Nagabana of Dakshina Kannada district.

Family: Succineidae

21. *Succinea baconi* (Pfeiffer, 1854)

Shell Size: Height=4-15mm, Width=3mm, No of whorls=3

Morphology: Shell small, thin, ovately conical, imperforate, flexuously striate, pale white, spire ,conical with a sharp apex; whorls rounded, rapidly increasing in size, last whorl large, angulately oval, peristome simple, columella with a very thin, narrow callus, rounded at the base.

Distribution: Throughout India

Ecology: Amphibious in nature, found near myristica swamps and coastal scrublands.

22. *Pupisoma evezardi* (Hanley and Theobald, 1874)

Shell Size: H= 2-2.5 mm, W= 1.5 mm, No. of whorls 5.

Morphology: Shell imperforate, with scarcely even a trace of rimation in the umbilical region, conoidly ovate, thin, horny, with raised hair like oblique lines irregularly disposed, on all the whorls. Spire nearly cylindrical below, conoidal above, suture impressed. Whorls convex; increasing regularly; the last but one larger than the penultimate, rounded at the periphery and below. Aperture diagonal, nearly circular, but truncated above, peristome thin, all in one plane, slightly expanded, margins converging; columellar vertical above, slightly twisted below, reflected and united to the whorl so as completely to cover the umbilicus.

Distribution: Western Ghats: Karnataka: Nagarholé, Sharavathi Valley, Nagabanas.

Family: Chronidae

23. *Kaliella barrakporensis* (Reeve, 1852)

Shell Size: Height= 2.4-3.6mm, Width= 2-3mm, No. of whorls=6-7

Morphology: These are microgastropods with shells are translucent and thin silky lustre .The trochiform pale brown shell has impressed sutures and about six slightly convex, slowly increasing whorls, with a peripheral keel on the last whorl, which is not descending. Several distinct, fine, oblique radial riblets are present on the whorls. The shell has a simple peristome with a straight and thin outer lip, even in adult specimens, and its aperture is rectangular. The early whorls appear blackish brown on living snails, while the bottom whorls are dark dirty yellow with darker black brown patches, spots and stripes.

Distribution: Widely distributed throughout India.

Land snail species reported from Coastal Karnataka and Western Ghats of Karnataka.

SI. No	Species	Habitat	IUCN status
1	*M. dussumieri*	All terrestrial habitats	Not evaluated
2	*M. indica*	All terrestrial habitats	Not evaluated
3	*Macrochlamys* sp.	All terrestrial habitats	Not evaluated
4	*E. indica*	Reserve forests, Plantations,Gardens	Not evaluated
5	*E. acuducta*	Gardens, Plantations	Not evaluated

6	*M. coeloconus*	Reserve forests, semi-forested regions	Not evaluated
7	*P. nanus*	Reserve forests, High altitude regions	Not evaluated
8	*Cyclophorus* sp 1.	Reserve forests, Plantations	Not evaluated
9	*Cyclophorus* sp 2		
10	*A. immerita*	Reserve forests	Not evaluated
11	*D. expatriatus*	Reserve forests	Not evaluated
12	*A. gracile*	Plantations, gardens	Not evaluated
13	*S. octona*	Greenhouses, Plantations, gardens	Not evaluated
14	*L. fulica*	All terrestrial habitats including urban areas	Least concerned
15	*Glessula* sp. 1	On ground, under the shade of large trees. Plains and hills, Forests, Cashew plantation, Nagabana of Udupi	Not evaluated
16	*Glessula* sp. 2		
17	*G. bicolor*	Agricultural lands, vicinity of human habitations	Not evaluated
18	*R. praetermissus*	Nagabana of Dakshina Kannada district	Not evaluated
19	*P. evezardi*	Nagabanas of Dakshina Kannada district	Not evaluated
20	*K. barrakporensis*	Plantations, Nagabanas, Forests, Gardens	Not evaluated
21	*S. baconi*	Closer to water bodies some arboreal living under the bark of trees, some on rocks	Not evaluated
22	*L. alte*	Lives in moist places, dry areas, mostly at lower altitudes	Not evaluated
23	*Rishetia sp.*	Gardens	Not evaluated

List of land snail species collected from the plantations of coastal Karnataka.

Species	Plantations						
	Arecanut	Banana	Coconut	Acacia	Cashew	Casurina	Rubber
M. dussumieri	+	+	+	-	+	-	+
M. indica	+	-	-	+	-	+	-
Machrochlamys sp	-	-	-	-	-	-	+
A. gracile	+	+	+	-	+	+	-
E. indica	+	-	-	-	-	-	+
E. accuducta	+	-	-	-	-	-	-
S. octona	+	-	-	-	-	-	-
L. fulica	+	-	-	-	-	-	-
L. alte	+	-	-	+	-	-	+
Cyclophorous sp 1	+	-	-	-	-	-	-
Glessula sp 1	-	-	-	-	+	-	-
G. bicolor	+	-	-	-	-	-	-
S. baconi	+	-	-	-	-	+	-
K. barrakporensis	-	-	-	-	-	-	+

* +: Present, -: Absent

Land snails of Karnataka: 1. *Allopeas gracile* 2.*Subulina octona* 3. *Lissachatina fulica* 4. *Rishetia* sp 5.*Glessula* sp1   6.*Glessula* sp. 2   7. *Macrochlamys indica*   8. *Macrochlamys* sp 9. *Rachistia praetermissus* 10.*Ariophanta immertia* 11.*Gulella bicolor* 14. *Pupisoma evezardi* 12.*Micraulax coeclonus* 13. *Dicharax expatriatus* 16. *Euplecta indica* 17.*Euplecta accuducta* 18.*Clyclophorous* sp.1 19. *Clyclophorous* sp.2 15.*Succinea baconi* 20.*Kaliella barakporensis* 21. *Pterocyclus nanus* 22. *Mariella dussumeiri* 23.*Laevicaulis alte* Scale bar: 3mm

Bibliography

1. Aravind N.A and Jadhav A (2023).Edible non marine molluscs of India. ATREE, Bangalore, ISBN: 9788196060695.

2. Aravind, N.A., Patil, R.K., and Madhyastha, N.A. (2008). Micromolluscs of the Western Ghats, India: Diversity, distribution and threats. *Zoosymposia*, volume 1 http://dx.doi.org/10.11646/zoosymposia.1.1.17.

3. Borges LS., Treneman NC., Haga T., Shipway J., Raupach M J., Altermark B., Carlton J T.(2022). Out of taxonomic crypsis: A new trans-arctic cryptic species pair corroborated by phylogenetics and molecular evidence, Molecular Phylogenetics and Evolution, Volume 166: ISSN 1055-7903.

4. Gauffre-Autelin P., von Rintelen T., Stelbrink B., Albrecht C. (2017). Recent range expansion of an intermediate host for animal schistosome parasites in the Indo-Australian Archipelago: phylogeography of the freshwater gastropod *Indoplanorbis exustus* in South and Southeast Asia. Parasit Vectors, 10(1):126.

5. Jayashankar M., Aravind N A., Reddy M., Reddy S. (2012). Distribution of pestiferous terrestrial molluscs in Bangalore region, Karnataka, Biodiversity and Taxonomy, Ed: A. Biju Kumar, M.P. Nayar, R.V. Varma and C.K. Peethambaran, Narendra Publishing House.

6. Madhyastha, N.A., Mavinkurve, R.G. and Shanbhag, S.P. (2004). Land snails of Western Ghats. In: Gupta, A. K.; Kumar, A. and Ramakantha, V. (Eds). Wildlife and protected areas, Conservation of rain forest in India, ENVIS Bulletin-4. 4: 143-151.

7. Mitra, S.C., Dey, A., and Ramakrishna. (2004). Pictorial Handbook Indian Land Snails (Selected species). *Zool. Surv. India*: 1-344.

8. Raheem D., Naggs F., Aravind N.A., Preece R.C.A. and Taylor H. (2009). An illustrated guide to land snails of Western Gats of India. Natural History Museum, London.

9. Ramakrishna and Mitra, S.C. (2002). Endemic Land Molluscs of India. Records in Zoological. Survey of India. Occ. Paper No. 196: 1-65 (Published: Director, Zoological. Survey of India. ISBN 81-85874-76-X.

10. Raut, S. K. and Goose, K. C. (1984).Pestiferous land snails of India. Technical Monograph, Zoological Survey of India pp.151.

11. Tripathi, B., and Mukhopadhayay, A. (2014). Freshwater Molluscs of India: An insight of into their diversity, distribution and conservation. Aquatic ecosystem biodiversity and challenges, 163-195.

Glossary

Caenogastropods: It is a taxonomic subclass of molluscs

Cannaliculate: Grooved or channeled longitudinally

Conoidal: Cone like

Crenulated: Wavy

Keel: Ridge or edge at the shoulder of the whorls

Ligament: The place of attachment of two valves of the shell

Paucispiral: Only slightly spiral, as in some opercula

Planospiral: A shell that is coiled in a single plane

Protoconch: Embryonic shell retained at the tip of the adult shell's spire

Spire: Top of the shell

Suture: The visible line that runs from the apex of the shell to the aperture